The poems in this collection draw upon the sounds, colours and quirks of urban and suburban Australia. Personal perceptions and associations are interwoven with snippets of speech, soundbites from TV shows, the percussive rhythm of highways and tramlines, and the atmospheric permutations of a climate in flux. Infused with a romantic sensibility, the poems dramatise the ways in which relationships are played out in ordinary circumstances, on balconies, backyards, streets and against skylines. As the poet exclaims, 'Oh Lord of Chlorine, Gear Sticks,/ Forklifts and Cream Cheese, forgive my short attention span./ Grant me a chance to find enchantment in ordinary things.' At the heart of the collection, the extended sequence of poems 'Golden Repair' portrays the intoxicating highs of love and the darker emotions that come with its loss – the anger, the recriminations, the loneliness. As a doctoral student, Carter studied Luke Davies' collection *Totem* – *Golden Repair* may be seen as her own extended outcry of praise and lament.

Carter shows compelling formal variety, a fine ear for the winning phrase, and an ability to coordinate seemingly disparate aspects of contemporary life, from the private to the public, the spiritual to the economic.
Assoc. Prof. Sean Pryor

LOUISE CARTER

GOLDEN REPAIR

NEW POEMS

First published 2023
from the Writing and Society Research Centre
at Western Sydney University
by the Giramondo Publishing Company
PO Box 752
Artarmon NSW 1570 Australia
www.giramondopublishing.com

Cover and design by Jenny Grigg
Typesetting by Andrew Davies
in 9/15 pt Tiempos Regular

Printed and bound by Ligare Book Printers
Distributed in Australia by NewSouth Books

A catalogue record for this
book is available from the
National Library of Australia.

ISBN: 978-1-922725-47-9

The Giramondo Publishing Company acknowledges the support
of Western Sydney University in the implementation of its book
publishing program.

This project has been assisted by the Commonwealth Government
through the Australia Council, its arts funding and advisory body.

For Nan

Contents

Pleasure in Elysium 1
Hot Clouds 2
Two Beer Pool Day 3
Goldsbrough 5
Commute 7
Limited Time Only 8

Golden Repair 11

The Come Down 33
The Rainbow Bird 35
Amaranthine 37
My Friend's Mum 38
We'll Get Stoned on the Couch If It Takes All Night 40
Mesmerised: 42
Ozzified 43
Marrickville 45
Honey 47

Bags of Flavour 48
Travels and Travails 50
Arlington 51
Perspective 52
Tramsheds 53
Body Worlds 54
Funeral 55
Cairns 58
Beverley Hills, New South Wales 59
Aubade 60
Mount Pleasant Avenue 61
History of Sadness 64
Windows 67
Foothills 69
Half Here 72

Notes 75
Acknowledgements 77

Pleasure in Elysium

A man with a bundle of balloons in his arms
Small feet that skim the darkened fairground
She'll lift you to heaven if you give her a chance
The tantrum of summer relinquishing heat

Small feet that skim the darkened fairground
Nonchalant as an arcing crow
The tantrum of summer relinquishing heat
Clouds of ink in calm dispersal

Nonchalant as an arcing crow
Diving for coins in a pool in a dream
Clouds of ink in calm dispersal
Come on, get your things, it's time to go home

Diving for coins in a pool in a dream
I will not encourage others to fly
Come on, get your things, it's time to go home
All dancers must follow the direction of grace

I will not encourage others to fly
A man with a bundle of balloons in his arms
All dancers must follow the direction of grace
She'll lift you to heaven if you give her a chance.

Hot Clouds

Hatching in hutches: the opaline budgies are abundant.
Pen etchings measure progress: your auntie is only five feet.
Funny words turn to fuzzy growls in the plastic heart of a bear.
Margarine sets over boiled potatoes like industrial varnish.

Pets excelling at pro chess: a border collie takes your queen.
The cold bone-white salt shaker fits cleanly in your hand.
Manatees sojourn in archipelagos, muscled and varnished.
Antique yellow like apple juice, whisky or sun shards.

The lone wild alligator rips off the tourist's feeding hand.
Car parts and sump oil. Screwdrivers. Specimen jars.
Antivenin is duly injected into the victim's arm.
Sit in soap milk until pink. Hot clouds in the cold green.

Larking galahs fly heavenward in feathered arcs.
Through a tear in a makeshift corrugated roof: the sky.
Milk drips from a goat's chin. Sheep wear crowns of cream.
Competing for the heater: singed ginger, smoky fur.

In the dense tangle of strangulated tree roots: an eye.
Fledging finches in gold light. Eternity. Abundance.
Releasing all of her secrets in serious croaky whispers.
Sunlight blurs. The birdcage is open, the yard bare.

Two Beer Pool Day

Tippy-toe sprinting down hot brick steps, yelping
as gumnuts embed themselves – the bloody things
always waiting with pointed ends up like thumbtacks
to trip us, no matter how many times Mum sweeps.

The obstacle course continues with the pool's Pebblecrete
rim, the enemy of skin, necessitating Dettol containers
nearly as large as the bulk-size chlorine buckets
we're prone to prising open and jabbing with sticks.

You can hear the filter wheezing even from the kitchen
as the *chk chk chk* of the pool cleaner competes with the sound
of cicada tinnitus. *It's a two beer pool day*, Dad declares
before dropping his pager in. *Not again, shit!*

Our neighbour's tree with its twitchy pipe cleaner branches
ensures the water's never clear – one time,
over winter, a family of ducks took up residence
on its dark green surface, much to my mother's chagrin.

But today it's blue as it'll ever be and Dad is wearing
speedos and easing himself into the Aqua Duck
with his beer, while my sister and I dare each other
to take a running jump and dive straight in.

For hours in the endless light of summer evenings
I would dive down deep as possible and stay there as long
as possible, admiring the world through water.
It was how I preferred to experience life: distorted.

Goldsbrough

The Gravity
of the Situation: you could walk around Sydney
on a muggy Spring day and everything falls like lead,
it seems like everyone's gone away and this could be
the edge of the world, and you the world's last person.
Luke Davies

The past is a multistorey car park. On weekdays
the city hums with sleepwalking workers, dutifully
constructing society's dream. From our balcony
in Pyrmont we saw rows of milky headlights
through iron bars – the smoke from our joints
shrouding their windshields. Heaviness set in –
the awareness that we're always falling.
Buildings and bodies eventually disappear,
but feelings remain like something you can hear.
It was autumn: a time when the Earth
turns away from the sun like a face cast downwards
away from love. We sat with each other in silence,
dumb in the day's accusatory whiteness,
immortal because the moment was endless –
suspended like static electrons trapped inside
a TV. The past is not behind but *beside* us,
an infinite horizon, and when the mind is quiet,
the sound will drift across like bells
or chimes. That balcony was part of Goldsbrough:
a warehouse built long ago for the wool trade
but turned into flats in the last twenty years
to store Sydney's surplus of people. The past

once felt exactly like the present – you can't go back
but you can treat the here and now with reverence.
Everything will be okay – I thought I had heard
the voice of God, but perhaps it was this poem, today.

Commute

Bursting through the crust of the Earth,
the train surfaces after Wynyard
and continues northwards along the bridge.

The sky's that clichéd shade of blue
painted aquamarine as if by crayon.

Sunlight flickers inside the carriage
like a film reel. Of all the commuters,
I'm the only one looking out the window.

I sit there and think about the theory
that says this world is necessarily perfect
and all things are in balance
and the meaning of existence is plainly evident
in the passage of time and the passing of seasons.

Then I realised I'd caught the wrong line
so I got off at Chatswood and waited,
while my thoughts meandered downstream
to the more pertinent question of dinner.

Limited Time Only

Her arse upon the clock hand like a builder
on a steel beam at lunchtime: tin pail filled
with sandwiches. The threat of the free-fall
can only instil fear for so long – eventually
the bored worker becomes inclined to tricks
such as poetry instead of sales copy: a call-
to-action written in metered prose, replete
with highfalutin adjectives. Nothing to lose:
no mortgage, no kids, not even a cat to feed,
she walks the length of hours and minutes
like Philippe Petit dancing above Manhattan
on a piece of wire – unreachable. The shriek
of a whistle as one shift ends and another
begins. She curtsies in mid-air; disappears.

Golden Repair

Saturdays can be so ordinary. When I was filling out the forms before I muscled my way out of my mother, nearly killing her, I ticked all the wrong boxes and wound up here. You were a twin: you've always had a touchstone. People speak of lightning when they want to describe a moment of destruction or inspiration: they say *struck* as if touched by the statically charged finger of some divine being. Out in the valley that night you were like an antenna, goading electricity. People also use the phrase *our paths were crossed* to describe a chance encounter. Our paths were crossed like the wires of a bomb. There was nothing chance about it.

You waited for me to turn up and then when I did
we said yes to each other almost immediately
and the roof disappeared from your Lotus Elise
the sky so ecstatically blue
every pop tune a hymn.
What men really want is a classy freak
a guy on Oprah once said as the audience cheered
and it was not foolish to think ourselves invincible
because you are when you look love straight in the eye
and wink. You teased me that time when we kissed
and you felt what I was feeling
and you said *which one of us will say it first?*
before teasing we could say it at the same time
as I flailed and squealed all that joy
bunched up like a painful sneeze.
Blueness a gas flame in that hot summer
and sunlight abundant, abundant
in the blue time of brightness
that stretched upwards and through us forever
a bright blue thread through our hearts and heaven.

Kintsukuroi (金繕い 'golden repair'): *The Japanese art of fixing broken pottery with lacquer dusted or mixed with powdered gold. As a philosophy it treats breakage and repair as part of the history of an object, rather than something to disguise.*

When I'm very drunk I sometimes start imagining
that in a past life I was a gay man who was murdered in the Eighties,
my gin and tonic still cold. A weakness for beauty and pop music,
I was seduced by *The Lexicon of Love* on an expensive stereo
by a gorgeous man who maybe didn't mean to kill me
but who trapped my breath beneath his pressing fingers
in a moment when, in fairness, I was eager to leave.
Here again in female form, delighted by my contours,
I'm weirdly drawn to nightscapes, balconies –
the whiff of cigarette smoke in air-conditioned hallways
in peach-coloured concrete apartment buildings.
Imagine my indignation when in the next life, he dumped me.
Not again, he muttered as our shoulders smacked
and our eyes met while he hovered, shaking his head,
dragging behind him the air of a ghost. *Why not this time?*
I yelled. *It's your turn to suffer.* Angry as youth denied immortality,
I threw lightning at him in poetry while he hid behind his leather sofa
until nothing was left but scorched memories
and pages and pages of anguished scribbling.

Of men
Nan says:
bullies
and wimps.

Meeting my Muse at last, he is a graceful opponent.

Have you eaten all the salt & vinegar, you cunt?

There are powerful personalities interacting here, and
there will be a tussle.

Baby, do I look flaccid enough?

Blood in its gums, sinew on its tongue.

Little geek girls, they're everywhere.

Walking around in love; a ball gown made of fishes.

I'm still trashed, so I wouldn't trust my opinion.

Updrafts of warm air; this is a winged descent.

Wanker

he says, unaware that I'm writing spells.

When you visit a nudist retreat, there comes a point –
after you've handed over your deposit to a sun-bleached woman
wearing only a singlet, her flat brown breasts visible –
where you actually have to take off your clothes.
Mid-afternoon, late summer – it all seemed feasible
until I saw the caretaker outside raking leaves,
his wrinkled testicles swinging like a pendulum.
Then panic, hysteria. It was our first fight of many
in the three days we spent there – I wanted to ease into it
but you demanded obedience. Walking outside
without clothing produces a cognitive dissonance
so fierce that *like a dream* becomes the only means of description –
I saw myself pale and wobbly walking through the bush
dressed only in sneakers, sunlight on my nipples,
trailing after your tan backside, cock ring glinting.
We took photos of each other on a big rock beside the creek
where we'd just seen the disappearing tail of a platypus.
It was a novel alternative to my office job, at least.
That night in our cabin you made me cook burritos
still nude; as dangerous as it was humiliating.
You were baiting me. I was exhausted. You started drinking:
It makes me mean. So I snapped and you pounced –
I think? I can't remember clearly. The only way back
is through the flesh – it's true that the body never forgets –
specifically, the cinch of the rope round my waist
as I entered the survival space where it's not about pleasure
but the strung-out bared-teeth sharpness
and grunt and clench of ghosts treating our bodies
like stolen cars in a deserted country town – thunder
explosions in the *Blair Witch* tempest that screeched down

around us, rain hurled like rice by dead relatives
at our black wedding – these are the places we went
together; these are the places I can’t forget.

When will this cycle of suffering end? the mind asks
at 3 a.m., convinced that it can solve any issue
as if life were a Rubik's cube or a game of Lemmings –
All in good time, the voiceless voice
of wisdom says. I've heard it said
the most important lessons are those
you need to learn and relearn
perpetually which is why I keep falling
for arseholes I guess and although John Lennon
insists that war is over if you want it
I enjoy fighting more than I'm prepared to admit –
like that time when you called me fat
and I called you a hypocritical old pig
and your face broke open into sudden bliss:
A girlfriend, a real *girlfriend I can* fight *with!*
as I stood with my suitcase half-packed
dinner half-cooked in your kitchen
rage like smoke from a saucepan boiled dry
not knowing whether to punch or kiss you
which is to say I miss you: our time together
like burning magnesium – gone in a white flash.

Déjà vu – the sense of physically inhabiting
a vision you had in childhood.
At fourteen I made the decision
to change schools; pursue dance.
It was doomed but I had to do it. I had to.
Fifteen years later, incapable
of learning from failure, I ventured
out from safety into danger
and there you were, waiting.
When people talk of hunger as coming
from the bones, they're right – we acquiesce to life
by eating. But thirst comes from the blood.
My journal entry from the first time we kissed:
He tasted of water.
My mum listens to AM radio
to mask the sound of her mind thinking
and once we heard a news story of a man
whose wife and children had died in a burning building.
How does a person recover from that? I asked.
They don't, she said – ten years before
her own divorce consigned most of her past
to silence.
You only did
what you needed to do and to hold a grudge
would be childish. From the ravaging wildness
of extreme places, I'm crawling towards quietness.
Eternity is not out there on the periphery
of the universe: it's inside us.

Silence, hello. Whatever I throw at you bounces back, so I'm trying to shut up but fuck, fuck – sometimes it's like surgery without anaesthesia and not being able to yell. *Better out than in* my dad would say whenever I wanted to chuck. I told my lovers to get stuffed in the last month and alone in this room of mirrors there's never enough gin to make that clown with the megaphone drunk enough to pass out. I imagine myself curled against a body I'd turn away from in the flesh. Easy to blame unhappiness on another person or their absence – far trickier to open the door to your gloomy guest and serve him a piece of cake. In the shower at 2 a.m. in an acid haze a voice asked if I was ready to stop hurting myself. Good question. Seems hypocritical to ask for kindness until I'm able to say yes. So I'm trying. I'm trying.

Come on, come and stand with me on this podium
for a minute – don't try to tell me you don't like it.
You were a public figure in the Nineties,
before you started hiding. If you're feeling naked,
here are some labels: Maltese, bisexual,
Sagittarius, activist, sadist. Computational,
you pay attention to data patterns.
You joked about how you fuck both genders
but prefer to have relationships with women
because you hate yourself. You tried to tell me
you were a psychopath – as if being tied up
and threatened with a knife did not make it
obvious – but I was a kind-hearted solipsist
and I didn't really believe in evil.
Now that I've done the reading, I'm choosing
to think you wanted very badly not to have
feelings, and for the most part you succeeded.
Perhaps those with Cluster B personalities
truly don't deserve love. They're empty,
says the literature. But you gave back.
You felt bad. I wasn't the helpless lamb
you initially wanted to kill and eat.
Now there's a hole where a whole life
could have been. It doesn't matter
anymore. I'm just crediting my source.

Perhaps all those melancholy children
have unfinished business from previous
lives – they died without finding their grail
only to respawn inside the game with no choice
but to give it another try. Finding you after so long
on the other side was reverse sadness –
a lightening. If God is love and you're prone
to taking things literally, a truculent older man
will do the trick – you gave and took like a flood
or firestorm, leaving my landscape bare
but fertile. Exponents of cognitive behavioural therapy
say that the path to stability is to learn to love
differently – to analyse the patterns that have led
to unhappiness and then consciously supplant
feeling with reason. They claim the rulebook
of life can be grasped by the mind, and to feel
your way forward with hands and not eyes
is a kind of wilful blindness. They're probably
right. In primary school I learned about
a convict who saved his rations for a week
then ate them all in one sitting and died
from a burst stomach. The question
arises: why am I still whining?
I'll drop to my knees and kiss the ground
as long as it takes for you to find whatever,
whomever can bring you to life.
You're not yet done. I wish you life.

Nasi goreng: every bachelor has a dish
to impress the ladies – your version
was scrumptious. My tastebuds cling
to the memory, a sensory haunting –
and through Sydney still I take myself
on expeditions to Indonesian restaurants
in search of lost rice.
                    That other version
of myself, the *Sliding Doors* Louise,
is probably gobbling food with you
at this moment, watching the news,
wondering what would have become
of the girl who dared to say *no* on the night
she heard the words: *move in with me*.
          What would I
and this other Louise discuss
if we were to meet? *Enjoy the sex
and the nasi goreng*, I'd tell her.
She'd smile. *Enjoy being free.*

Trod in cat poo with bare feet in darkness

May the Lord make me truly thankful

My right hand was broken, so I had to clean up one-handed

May the Lord make me truly thankful

Met the perfect guy on Tinder, who turned out to be a narcissist

May the Lord make me truly thankful

Found a vocation that brings fulfilment but not an income

May the Lord make me truly thankful

Re-typed the 'thankful' refrain instead of copy/pasting

Because the process is important

May the Lord make me truly thankful; in gratitude the heart stays open.

I'm on a forgiveness spree – my pen not a sword
but a magical wand, and solemn in my wizardry,
I anoint the heads of all the many men who've ever
annoyed me. After all, aren't men just manifestations
of ego – absurd and contemptible, yet poignant
in their vulnerability – what kind of warrior
would I be to eviscerate such easy targets?
C'mon, Louise, let the poor creatures be,
let your grievances disperse like smoke
in clean country air. The thing I've learned
is you can get your chakras cleared and quit drugs
and smoking and drinking and eat nothing but steamed
organic broccoli – but within the rancorous embers,
something still seethes. I recall the look
on your ex-girlfriend's face when we saw her
at that exhibition – *wounded pride* I called it,
feeling superior. It's been three years
since you turned me loose. Time can heal
but to speed up time with substance abuse
is cheating. Coming down on your couch
on New Year's Day. The feeling of finding
something you've lost but have forgotten
to search for. A word surfaces: *surrender*.

The percussive urban static of dry leaves and grit,
like the sound of a texta marking an X through another
calendar day. I'm placing a copy of *A Suitable Boy*
on the shelf – trying to create space for its largeness.
The shelves heave with time, with entire lives
spent in blinkered pursuit of the next line
only to end up with their souls trapped inside
a dog-eared paperback with a broken spine
that will someday get culled to make room
for the recent winner of the Booker Prize.
This bookstore is alive with the dead.
I'd close up early but I need the extra dollars
and cents because I've given up on capitalism
but not hedonism which is inconvenient because
man, what a combo! So it's another night of cheap wine
and Pad Thai made with cage eggs which I eat while I think
about my credit debt in between checking my phone
for messages that will never be written, let alone sent.
I'm caught between thinking that loneliness is a mental state
that you need to learn how to transcend; or it's the very thing
that propels us into the discomfort of adventure –
the motivator that drives existence onward.
Lying in bed, I'm struck by my polarised approach
to the question. Reading is not the same as meditation –
it's a voluntary inhabitation of someone else's head.
I write so others may know what you were so keen to forget.

Before you, the ex with his flag planted at the peak
of my psyche was a dyslexic who dragged me
kicking and screaming into adulthood.
I had thought those highs were unrepeatable,
but then you came along and cauterised
my entire sense of past and future
like ECT – leaving me burnt out and shuffling
through a static wasteland of memory.
The thing that's dumb about being hung up
on your silence is that communication
is often thwarted by speech. I've also come
to appreciate that truly knowing someone
is not possible through the Vaseline-smeared lens
of love – you need the clarity that distance brings
and you need compassion to realise that no one
is perfect. I know that you wanted us to work,
and I know you have suffered. I'm sorry.

Lovely girl said the man at the servo.
Never even looked at his face – I wanted
to go home, to be alone – *Have a good night*
I said as I strode past him, fled.
So here I am
on the back porch, smoking cigarettes,
writing poems to my loneliness
on another unfulfilling weekend.
Lovely girl he said.
Saw my mother today from the other side
of a roast chook – *I'll have a leg.*
She's a person, of course
not a mythical figure of birth and death,
and cannot answer all the questions
I could ever ask about why
or what next, so we talk about
the deliciousness of the stuffing instead.
You're a person too, of course
not an angel or devil; not the entry point
to eternity that once you were. And all
for the best, except for the thoughts that swing
like doors in and out of parallel worlds
in which we are immortal and breathing love again.
Such moments of pause
feel like hallways – a thoroughfare in an airport –
watching planes take off and land through windows
as I stumble back and forth between airport bars,
listening for my name on the PA system.
Air conditioning desiccates
the skin. The toilet paper in these airport bathrooms

is too thin. My mouth has a dryness that bottled water
        cannot quench.
        Lovely girl he said.
You were my spiritual twin –
a wounded healer, and whenever you were able
to disengage your ego, we were for each other
like kidneys, filtering sadness and pain.
        I'm famished,
but these airport burritos are overpriced
and tasteless. Perhaps that's why they call it 'missing' –
your plane is on the runway but you're stuck
in a food court or toilet, and the air hostess is calling
your name but you're too self-absorbed or lovelorn
                to notice.

Are we there yet? I hope so.
I don't want to wear the uniform
of the eternally broken-hearted – these words
like birds beneath a woollen coat, fighting
for freedom. I'm so sick of talking
to myself I want to throw this conversation
to somebody else.
I can see the future and it's not perfect
but what is? I'll give this morning
my dirty muddled human blessing – I'll give
this mourning my dirty muddled human
blessing – I'll give these birds back to the world:
may they sing.

The Come Down

Olive green blurring to dirt and the sky white as paper.
Currawongs. Isolation.
Tree branches curled in brace position
and leaves with tips like seismometer needles
in the awestruck eye of morning.

The night before we'd driven up a steep ramp
to oblivion, drawn heavenwards by music.
I'd written down what I could hear.

Waking up behind the wheel
with moon dust on the windshield, caking us in.
We burst out into bushland and saw a bird,
rare as a platypus, with AstroTurf plumage
and a traffic cone beak. Our totem.

It could only be auspicious.
We would marry each other and buy a hut out here,
call it 'Glue'. I'd set up a typewriter
and write poetry nude. We'd have children.
They'd be tan-skinned, like you.

The bird flew into the sky and pierced its glass.
Ice rain peppered the ground; ice shrapnel.
From the deck we watched a wallaby hop
like a soldier who'd wandered into no-man's-land

as, for minutes and minutes and minutes
the snare drum sound of hailstones
cried war, war. It was a queasy beauty
and we watched, queasily, in silence, for minutes.

The wallaby gave up and huddled by a frail tree,
snout twitching, until the hail stopped.
Then it bounded off across a crystal carpet
bright in the sudden sun.

My notebook lay open from the night before
like a postcard to myself from space
but I didn't write about the bird or the hail;
I didn't have the ability.
I was a sculpture, shaped by your hands,
waiting to be fired in the furnace of our breakup.

You sculpted a bird and I was gratified to learn
the wings worked. They were useful
when you threw me out into the air
                                                            of my future.

The Rainbow Bird

for Anna-May

Her beauty's a lazy place to start,
it's so easy. How my gaze sinks in
like a cream pie projectile.
A springtime offering:
she is hay bales and peaches.
In a previous life, gingham.
                                        My Dorothy.

Sunshine like meteor fire – I'm asleep
in her bed of embers. Leaning down
through waxy bathwater to kiss her
alive. The thunderstorm internalised.

To be coaxed from the obituaries
by a loquacious child. An epileptic fit
of orange curls – the feminine
and the guttural.

                                        Afloat
in the same ripple. The birdseed
fall-away of a disintegrating sandbank –
my feet scramble for assurance to find
only water, a soda stream
of effervescence and a thrown
torch floating down through darkness.

The lorikeet with its head bent
sideways as if to ask:
where is she?

Amaranthine

There's a tree branch pressed against your window:
leaves flexed up, muscular and persistent.
Roots sunk deep into the marshy clay
sucking fecundity upwards, persisting, *breathe*.

A plastic fern in your empty fish tank
leans against the dusty glass as if in agreement.
When I see you, the room reverberates
with major chords, steamy as a greenhouse.

Enough to make a lugubrious old man giggle.
Swing-dancing into our allocated roles,
eerily synchronous as if we'd already rehearsed
the steps in another life, or in dreams.

Let's treat this like a memory we can walk
around in. The palace doors creak open onto
gilded wings: in every room an instrument.
We can stay forever. We are immortal here.

My Friend's Mum

'I once loved a hobo in the park.'
This was my friend's mum talking, her papery face
suddenly a lantern. I kept prattling
as if she'd said something ordinary, something
not quite so aligned with my own predicament.
A hobo in the park – my inner tape recorder
got it, even if my drunk mind didn't.
Her eyes were blue as a Sydney summer,
the same eyes that once treasured society's trash.
The stupidity of wisdom. I told my lover once:
'You'll end up like one of those guys in the park
you know, the ones who yell at nothing and throw
bottles at people.' We were in my car, driving
across the Harbour Bridge. 'I don't care!' he said,
a fresh burst of spit coating his week-old t-shirt
like air freshener, the cheap kind that's labelled 'Alpine'
in black letters, and smells even worse than shit.
It was 11.30 by the time we reached his office,
which is either shockingly late or 'Just in time
for lunch!' depending on whether your half-filled glass
contains vodka. At some point I suppose
I'll have to stop finding him hysterical
or I'll end up with the surname 'Jones'
and a bedroom with a leafy vista.
I know. But my friend's mum doesn't judge
because she knows the wilfulness of love,

the hurricane that howls in from nowhere,
from stillness to gale force in a breath.
Transient as we all are: voyeurs in a dream.

We'll Get Stoned on the Couch If It Takes All Night

We stripped him
ran a knife through his belly
shook the treasure out:

gold coins

guitar picks

misshapen cutlery

a bar coaster bearing two names:
Collette / Vickianne

Memories ransacked
we forced his rigid form
through the narrow doorway
in darkness, hushing each other
so the neighbours wouldn't hear.
Ten years of dust in our fingernails
leaving a crumb-trail behind us

of condom wrappers

soy fish

dirt

and more guitar picks

We shunted him down a concrete staircase
and out through the car park
to dump his gutted carcass
in front of someone else's house.

Back upstairs, we were confronted
by his vinyl imposter
still in its bubble-wrapped bondage.
Impassive, it watched
as we argued about screwdrivers
our sweat speckling the carpet

as if

from

a watering

can

But we got it upright
plonked our arses on it
drank wine, smoked weed
in silence; co-conspirators
in a breathless meantime.

Mesmerised:

the word derives from Mesmer,
a German guy who spoke of *animal magnetism*,
of energy transference. Mesmer, with his swirling
pinwheel eyes that paralyse the mind and slow down
time, the swoon on the cusp of an epiphany, a dream
that's neither good nor bad, but interesting.
Standing in my lover's light I'm caught
like a child in a doorway looking up at a giant
and his meanness dissolves as he carries me
like a tombola prize with my feet dangling
through the sky. But like so many boys he's rough
with his toys, and plastic can only be pushed so far
before it will snap. Yet whenever I crack
he's always the one to come back, waving
his wine-stained peace rag, his voice casting spells
and his eyes like magnets, electrified –
and the whole thing starts again.

Ozzified

Iceberg lettuce from a foggy crisper with a spike in the middle where the slightly brown stalk is impaled until the good bits are eaten and you're left with those vampiric foetal inner leaves that will sit there rotting for a week before someone sighing chucks it in the bin put some in a bowl toss it in SAXA salt and instant dressing the one you keep in the fridge door shake it up so it isn't just oil peel your baked potato from the copper-tinted foil top with pre-shredded cheese no need to gunk up your grater and grate off parts of your own fingers not to mention washing the bloody thing chews up sponges faster than the dog chews up those rubber toys that are supposed to be indestructible except your mutt has consumed at least three and pooped out bits of rubber for all the neighbours to see then we've got sauce the red sort you put on pies with gunk at the tip to which flies will stick some say it's too sweet but we have a word for those people and that's *weak* Tip Top sliced thin smeared with Flora or Meadow Lea pale yellow with serrated indentations and churned up crests of crumbs like a choppy swell full of sand and broken shells smear it on thick heat your barbie and sear your meat when it starts to smoke it's nearly done with sausages what you're looking for is a crunch steak should be grey and tough onions nicely charred pile it up with sour cream feel your plastic knife vibrate slipping past glistening chops into the coleslaw elbow pasta grated carrot white pepper back again for seconds fish for tinnies in the Esky ring pull

cracking like a trigger pink skin smokes and rum later on
going for a Maccas run hot fries in your thirty-cent cone
get it into ya nice aye

Marrickville

It's been three weeks since I cleaned the bathroom
and it hasn't been cleaned since. But that's what you get
in a share house – a glorified squat for people
who don't want to pay full rent but dress it up
as 'community mindedness' – a place where conversations
about the fairest division of the gas bill take place
over the compost bin. You could say, hopeful of heart,
that it's a family, which it is – dysfunctional –
the air seething with PMT, all of us rolling
out yoga mats to the sound of the kettle boiling,
the fridge stocked with kale and coconut water
but never meat. We're a generation of ideological orphans
building Zion in Marrickville, our dyed hair a symbol
of our kinship – while the other residents, the old-school
Greek immigrants, gaze bewildered from their porches
as we jog or cycle past. I'm so far from home,
from the buzz-cut lawns and yipping dogs, from kitchens
with microwaves and African violets softly dying
beside disinfected sinks. These days I take comfort
in YouTube and weed on nights when the urge
to give up on this poetry caper becomes overwhelming –
the fear that there's nothing you can do to avoid
becoming your mother so you might as well swallow
your insolence, move back to the suburbs and give birth
in front of the TV. These days I force my focus
onto whatever the present moment happens to reveal –

organic toothpaste, soup bowls caked with chia seeds,
my own face in the mirror – the intimate recognition
of a stranger in this, the mediocre immediate.

Honey

A short-term lover who kept bees for their honey
once called me a whore for writing advertising copy:
I disagreed. It's not prostitution, I countered.
Copy and poetry are different things;
I can't make money from art, but hey, I gotta eat.
While not keeping bees he worked full-time
as a middle manager and lived with his parents rent-free.
He asked which one of us I thought was smarter,
and chuckled smugly when I told him: 'me'.
For someone who'd built a career on selling things
I undersold myself for years, and for a supposed
sex worker, I was scandalously underpaid.
This guy was allergic to bee stings and every time
he tended his hives he risked dying.
Spend forty hours a week in church with your head bowed,
praying, and you'll start to feel religious –
you can only write propaganda for so long
before you start to believe it. I told myself
there was no other way to survive in this money-hungry life
and like a fearful wife, I stayed.
My eventual exit can't even be claimed as brave –
I was 'let go' for not being a 'team player'.
There was a time when I thought of my many failed relationships
in terms of waste – I gave the best parts of myself away
at bargain-basement prices. But what of my gains?
Sustaining a reader's attention is hard,
yet here we are. His honey tasted like love.

Bags of Flavour

What we want to see is *you* on a plate.
It's essential the meat's cooked *perfectly*.
What this dish lacks is a crunchy element.
That sauce has just got *bags* of flavour!
Time goes fast in the MasterChef kitchen.
You've gotta work hard to stay in the competition.

When you first entered this competition
did you ever think that one day you would plate
a dish like this in such a prestigious kitchen
where everything's gotta be cooked *perfectly*?
We're amazed by your ingenious flavour
combinations and the care you've given each element.

She's enjoying this cook, she's in her element
and hasn't she just come so far in this competition?
She's achieved incredible depth of flavour.
C'mon you've gotta admit this is a cracking plate
of food – that fish is just cooked *perfectly*.
It takes a lot of strength to survive in this kitchen.

But haven't we seen some *disasters* in this kitchen?
I just don't *understand* the vegetable element.
We told him the quail has to be cooked *perfectly*.
Things have really started to heat up in this competition.
The problems in the cook have shown up on the plate:
everything's sadly lacking in finesse and flavour.

Remember, if your dish doesn't deliver on flavour
this could be your last cook in the MasterChef kitchen!
Don't forget, you'll need time to plate
and make sure you season every element
because you don't want to leave this competition
on the back of a dish that isn't cooked *perfectly*.

What we want to see is a dish that's cooked *perfectly*
and absolutely jam-packed with flavour –
the stakes are higher than ever in this competition
and everyone's fighting for their place in the kitchen.
Make sure you taste each individual element
together with everything else that's on the plate.

Five! Cook it *perfectly! Four!* Season each element!
Three! Get it on the plate! *Two!* Stay in the competition!
One! Conquer the kitchen! *Time's up!* Give us FLAVOUR!

Travels and Travails

The arm of a shirt I paid seventy bucks for
when I didn't have the money is poking out
of the laundry pile as if hitching a ride
out of its slovenly neighbourhood.
In Sydney, the road *less travelled* is characterised
by potholes and speeding traps and brothels –
while those on the motorway glide homeward
in BMWs. The cost of a functioning e-TAG
is office work, open-plan: with Arnott's
Assorted and Tim Tams offered
in lieu of a work-life balance.
At my last job, kitchen duties were enforced
by printouts of attack dogs.
The CEO ran nineteen kilometres
before eating her Paleo breakfast each morning
and demanded our attendance
at compulsory yoga workshops.
Whenever a staff member would disappear
their name would be scratched off the cleaning roster.
On the day I was sacked
for not attending an unpaid team-building exercise
on a Saturday, the road on the drive home
seemed narrower. I can't go back.

Arlington

The high-rises were going up and the builders' dust
was blasting sideways every time a truck juddered past
in a flatulent rush. All night, the squeaking of axles
and the hollow thumps of rusted barrels –
I was striving for a noble silence but could only manage
tinnitus. The mind, like muscle, will eat itself
if not nourished. No wonder I was miserable.
So I moved from a grubby share house to another
grubby share house in the loveless chill
of a wintry spring and trekked mud through the carpet
on the day I moved in – the awning forming a prison
of rainwater. Boxes strewn through the kitchen,
I gazed out at a hulking mobile phone tower
behind the trees: *At least you'll get reception here?*
The nearest tram stop was Arlington – orderly
as a model train running through a miniature village.
Whenever I walked towards it, my body would shrink
along with my eardrums (or so it seemed) – as in dreams,
Arlington was muted; soundless. Trams would appear
in silence and I'd join their cargo of tiny people
to travel, like an epiphany, back to life's loudness.

Perspective

Heaviness and heat. There's no way around
the tourists – caught in their resinous inertia,
I slow to an otiose plod. Cigarette-butt confetti
adorns the kerbside where we wait for the green man
while the smell of cremation, barbecue-glazed,
wafts up from Hurricanes – the ribs place
where patrons eat with bibs. The sun
is a heat lamp, pressed to the roof of our terrarium.
Since October, the bridge across Darling Harbour
has been rigged with speakers so pedestrians can listen
to *Frosty the Snowman* on forty-degree days.
Christmas is inevitable, inexorable, more so
than death – no amount of running on a treadmill
can prevent it: the date is set. The conveyor belt
of days and weeks has been getting faster,
but within the day's oppressive slowness
is stillness – the sensation of time expanding
like hot glass, softly expanding: a wobbling
blister of breath. Skyscrapers have replaced
cathedrals as structures of grandeur and might,
and the hush of ducted air conditioning
is a kind of breathing. My office window frames
peace; I keep the blind open to see ugliness
recede. With time enough and distance,
suffering transmutes into wisdom. A plane glides
between buildings. All of us are loved.

Tramsheds

Those old trams were like wrecked ships in the swirling murk
of an underwater crypt. We passed through in shoals –
some with cameras, some with rope. To enter,
we'd break in through a hole in the fence, ignoring the sign,
rusted and bent: *TRESPASSING IS PROHIBITED* –
and pass from sparkling order into shadowy neglect.

Back then, in Glebe, us weirdos could afford the rent.
But much can change in a decade. The only trams now in this locale
are functional, modern, swift – transporting the Great Washed
to respectable jobs – the carriages defaced not with spray paint
but ads. The sheds are unrecognisable –
gentrified and desecrated – entry is via escalator.

It's *Sydney's Most Dynamic Food Destination*, but you can't get
a sandwich – the closest thing is a croque monsieur, topped
with a duck egg. The exposed kitchen reveals the chefs –
tattoo-embellished, ironically bopping to Elton John,
proud of their *ethical lifestyle choices*.
Sixteen bucks – the sandwich is oily, hard to eat and heavy.

Above the fluorescent overheads you can see the original rafters.
Up there, the architecture – once cutting-edge, now antiquated –
holds steady. Ten years ago, I realised there's no such thing
as permanence, only decoration. It was humbling and comforting.

Body Worlds

A travelling show of 'plastinated' human bodies
is passing through Sydney. The posters show a skinless man
arched like a dancer, with nerves and tendons fanned out
where there should be hands. His eyeballs seem to stare
right at you no matter where you stand; his expression
seems slightly sad, but maybe that's just my impression.
I saw one of these exhibits about twelve years ago:
on a date. It's hard to be flirtatious around flayed corpses
but I was infatuated, and the very strangeness of that day
has prevented the memory from fading. There was sadness
then too – even amid the romance – and the contorted
displays of human remains were flaking slightly
at their edges: the plastic was scuffed in places.
That's what my mind captured: gauzy filaments
at the end of what were once a person's fingers,
flickering in the air conditioning. I picture this image
now as I pass a billboard for the new exhibition
on my way to work. It's autumn again and the air
is perfumed with decomposition. It smells of change –
a mulchy bouquet that instructs animals to burrow.
A gust floods my senses and my feet become tiny:
encased in kid-sized gumboots, I crunch through huge
piles of orange leaves. Seems odd to say 'my'
when referring to the body of that child. Those cells
have long since been replaced. The sadness stayed.

Funeral

Lost my shit at a taxi that wouldn't let me merge:
callous Sydneysiders dominate the roads
at all times. It's not their problem if you're driving
to a funeral.
                    A guy in the chapel driveway guides my car
to improvised parking as if it were the Easter Show,
and I end up right in front of the door.
I want to keep a low profile: I didn't know
my great aunt Enid very well. These people
could be strangers –
                    yet they seem to know my name.
I'm terrified of small talk, especially
when wisecracking is off the cards.
There's a part of my brain dedicated to sabotage:
I want to laugh.
                    My sister and I are asked to share
a program. She's thirsty so I grab a bottle of water
branded with the funeral home's logo. We find seats
near the back just as an overly manicured lady
gets things started.
                    There's no coffin:
this is a 'celebration of life'. I'm relieved,
but aunt Lyndal is incensed – this is death
and we shouldn't try to pretend otherwise.
I'm transfixed by the ruched curtain
above the pulpit – I can't figure out if it's fabric
or concrete that's been painted salmon pink.

Eulogies are given.
Enid's parents came from England, she was their first
child, born in Penrith. They were farmers. My pop
was her brother – he wanted to study medicine
but that wasn't an option for the working class
at the time. His ambition was transferred
to my father.
I'm fine until the photo slideshow.
'Wind Beneath My Wings' plays, too quietly,
and I can't believe it's making me want to cry.
Actually I want to weep but I can't let go
even at a funeral: the one event in our culture
where crying is acceptable
if not required.
I feel so dreadfully sad and tired.
I want to weep, but I'm worried about smearing
my makeup and making some kind of scene,
so I stare at the ceiling and force it all
back in.
We can't drive away immediately
because everyone's been parked in by each other
so we mill around the car park, tear-streaked
but loosened with weird euphoria:
the tough bit's over, plus it's a Monday
and we're not at work. A teenage cousin
twice removed is wearing tight shorts –
I ask my sister if that's a funeral faux pas.
She nods. *Of course.*
The wake is at a golf club.
I'm heartened by the prospect of snacks,

and that's where I find my aunt and dad:
huddled round the sandwiches. I'm handed
a large glass of shiraz.
After all, Enid was partial to a tipple.
The sun has come out over the golf course, green
through the windows. It's the closest I've come
to touching bare earth today.
I invite Dad back
for trash TV and Uber Eats.
We share a bottle of red then I send him
to his hotel.
On the laser-printed Order of Service
a young Enid is smiling. I file her with my tax receipts.
Death and taxes. She doesn't mind; finds it amusing.
Dark humour runs in our blood: an epiphany.
Then, peace.

Cairns

Woolworths was odd. Sunscreen and chicken nuggets
right next to each other – everything a tourist could want.
In Cairns, asking for prosciutto is asking to be punched,
so bacon it was – too pink, sliced thick. Already on tour,
a premature honeymoon – we ate midnight chip butties
with our pants off. For three days we slept too late
and made love too long – the sheets and towels
were never washed and the bin filled with condoms.
Whenever we emerged in search of a bottle shop
there was music – acoustic duos crooning covers
in beer gardens, and children busking beside the lagoon.
The air smelled of barbecues. Shimmering particles
of mirrored dust made the mountains iridescent –
brightest at dusk. The sunsets seemed everlasting
because there was nothing to distract us from watching –
the sky passed from tipsy to feisty to black-out drunk.
We collected each other's secrets: an Easter-egg hunt.
Like plastic figurines stuck to the bottom of a snowdome
we were sealed in a bubble, oblivious and buffered –
snow could have fluttered down to our beach towels
and we wouldn't have noticed. Shouty headlines
about global warming and Donald Trump were muted
on the other side of a soundproof pane of glass,
and the plotlines of our family dramas were paused.
Bacon crackled in the pan. Like a silent call to prayer,
sacredness vibrated through the air. It changed us.

Beverley Hills, New South Wales

Google Maps reckons it's twenty minutes by car
but we want to get on the piss so we catch the train
from Kirrawee and change at Wolli Creek
where the sunlight refracts and our lips meet
clear easy spacious I've never been here before
Beverley Hills New South Wales might actually
be heaven yellowing diamonds spell the word
'CHEMIST' Chinese restaurants breathy traffic
civic bustle the air puffs and billows the bubble
grows larger we are translucent with kindness
there is time around us like lukewarm bathwater
we toddle softly brimful with wonder lucid
dreamers existing exactly where happiness is

Aubade

My gaze is a question
I can't stop asking
I don't mind waking
with the magpies now
light blazes a ring
round your curtains
you don't want to disturb
me I'm monstrous
but how can I remain
asleep I've reached
my destination at last
and jet-lagged
in this foreign place
that feels familiar
you pull me under
the sheet I'm sealed
inside muscle and flesh
my gaze is a question
your answer is always
yes

Mount Pleasant Avenue

December turns cross-eyed,
hallucinates purple: a blue rinse
that tints the Sydney skyline
while bees raid dying flowers
like dumpster divers and
storm drains clog.
                    You drive north across the bridge,
air con struggling in a dirt-caked car crammed
with cracked CDs. You've been driving
this thing for fifteen years, your friends
are strapping kids into SUVs, and you're still
listening to *Kid A*.
                    Mount Pleasant Avenue
actually almost lives up to its name. The day
flickers with glossy emerald tongues
and the light solidifies to powdered gold.
Around a gumtree-lined curve
there's street parking offering privacy
for pointless Insta scrolling;
you're stalling.
                    Yet a pale blue eye
makes contact through the passenger
window, a woman who has met
with time's arrow at exactly her middle,
bent over at a right angle,
a human hinge.

You have been seen.
No one is at reception, there's a bell
with a passive-aggressive tinkle
but little else. Just flower
arrangements and an antiseptic
smell. Down a carpeted hall
you huff, irritation masking
your fear.
A nurse emerges
from a wing, knows where your nan
is, sends you to a double-door lift.
Inside, more nurses huddle
round an iPhone, gushing over
photos of a newborn.
The door opens.
There's an empty sitting room with a piano
limply draped in tinsel. The only sound
is the tinny burble of televised cricket.
Your nan's room has an en suite
with inbuilt support rails and a minibar
stocked with lemonade: it could be the Hilton,
if you really squint.
She's anxious again.
They were meant to bring her pills at 3 p.m.
but it's 3.10. You press the call button and wander
ineffectually down the hall under the pretext
of helping. Finally a nurse appears,
a kind Filipina. *How are you, Mrs Carter?*
She smiles.

You can picture her scooping
up a screaming child, cheerfully soothing
it as it cries, with the compassionate
detachment of a natural. Pills taken,
Nan says she's tired, needs a lie down,
there's no need for you to stay.
She's lying
but you play along, help her take off her shoes,
say goodbye. Gum leaves stream round the sides
of your car as you drive away. She had your dad
at nineteen, back when that's what women did.
Your life path wasn't quite so prescribed:
spoiled, you fritter, drift.

History of Sadness

The window frames a pink dusk, dot-matrix
through the fly screen. 'Miraculous' is a bit much

but it's been nearly a season without sky.
Smoke-choked for so long, I'm a child noticing

God for the first time. Bat silhouettes
pass overhead in wobbly trajectories.

I call Steven from his scrubbing to watch
the swirling lilac and silver curlicues of cloud:

a magic trick, or prophecy. Our eyes are still
wet. He's intent on tricking the bats, clapping

to send them off course. The heady stench
of jasmine is aggressively feminine. Petals

stream. I'm not clucky so much as I'm tired
of grief. Each month the history of sadness

congregates inside me; virulent. Ants swarm
toilet paper and tissue boxes; I reach for a Kleenex

and smear myself with peppery energy.
Jesus. The dishwasher clicks and shushes.

I could pray, but I'm not sure what to ask for.
They're seeking fig trees and sex. In a café I asked

a Magic 8-Ball if everything would be okay
and it replied: *YES*. There's an old cockatoo

that's been coming around, skeleton-grey
and mangey; the other birds squawk it away.

Maybe it was a cruel person in another life;
this is how I justify my actions when I spray

mosquitoes and wasps. But don't bad people
start as children who've been traumatised?

I wanted to end the cycle. Grief is an addict,
pleading. You'll do anything. I wasn't arguing

with Steven; I saw his side and agreed with it.
There's an inner misalignment, like a car tire

that veers away from the highway. Hot nights
dreaming of still-alive cats and ballet exams.

Sweat: the body crying. Struggling up staircases
on torpid days. Unconquerable laundry hampers.

Then change. Cool air. Relief. Rain.
While sorting underpants, I get a response

of sorts. *Pay attention to whatever* isn't *pain.*
The room expands with subdued brightness.

Windows

Four straps over one shoulder: the usual
baggage, plus a blood pressure monitor.
At twenty-minute intervals it beeps
and constricts, measuring my blood
as it struggles through tunnels.
                                        Hypertension:
a gift from my stressed ancestors.
I remember my pop scraping every last skerrick
of wine from a foil cask with a metal ruler
and Nan's salty treats – Lay's Thins –
stashed on top of the fridge. Our hearts
and brains are prone to blowing up.
                        I'm trying to stay calm
but I've just climbed four flights
to my boyfriend's apartment to discover
one of the keys I had cut is a dud.
It's lunchtime and I need to pee.
The machine grips my arm like a floatie
inflated by an overzealous parent
                                  with Olympian lungs.
Through the smudged vestibule window
I can see across town, where my friend Tamara
is currently dying. It's a process: an unspooling
list of things she'll never do again, grieved
in real time.
          Seemingly mundane milestones
like birthdays take on weight – she cried

to realise she wouldn't reach my age:
thirty-eight. Talking about the future
feels like a faux pas, and attempting to relate
is met – quite rightly – with scorn.
The pain disrupts her sleep, denying her
even that escape into ignorance.
When I leave her place
I feel guilty relief. But a livestream
in my mind plays in a browser window
where her sunken eyes connect with mine
and ask to be witnessed.
Standing outside
Steven's locked front door, I picture all
the boring things I would do in there:
make tea, defrost bread, open my laptop
under the pretext of poetry or work
only to scroll news sites and social media
and get increasingly depressed.
I leave my bags
and go back to the street: a frigid wind tunnel
of weekday efficiency. Pensioners in masks
mill outside the medical centre.
Office workers queue for chicken rolls.
I sit beneath the last remaining red leaves
of a Japanese maple, trying to resist the pub.
A month later I'll buy a Fitbit
and my blood pressure will go down.
At Tamara's bedside I'll check my step count
while neighbours on nearby balconies
take pictures of the setting sun.

Foothills

Nothing wrong with memorialisation said Kate Fagan
as she handed my drafts back. Nothing wrong
with dipping memories in the hot plastic of poetic language
except they turn into trinkets.
                                        It was a backhander
from a professional player who smashed
their protégés to strengthen their game.
                                                Sensing my dismay,
she went on to say my work was in the foothills of Ashbery.
Ashbery! I exclaimed as she firmly repeated, *foothills.*
Foothills! Too late: my head had already outgrown
the door and it took half an hour with a hacksaw
to get me out of her office. I was new to poetry
and infatuated: the heavens and I were in conversation.
Ah, those were the days.
                                Ashbery, that trickster
whose scriptures were administered to undergrads
majoring in creative writing to test their dedication.
In a windowless classroom at UTS I sat in a square of desks
staring at my photocopied excerpt of 'Flow Chart'
willing it to make sense. When Martin Harrison asked
what we thought the poem was about
we mumbled answers that seemed safe – Time?
Intransience? The seasons? Bees? – he nodded
with a sly grin before revealing
it wasn't meant to make sense
in any particular way. It was Ashbery's reaction

to his mother's death: a textual savannah
of mannered calmness. Those undulating stanzas
glinted like fish but I preferred Martin's own work
for its clarity and stillness. When he read to us from *Summer*
I could *see* it as if the images were projected
against the wall of that boxy room, summoning
the lapping water of a swimming pool:

> *It has coolness, too, greyness and limpidity,*
> *together with the slight echo of pre-traffic moments*
> *shimmering across its transparence, its daybreak light.*

Now it's summer again
and I'm watching my houseplants wriggle
in the oscillations of a Kmart fan while the kitten
I found in a drain ten days ago splays on the couch,
breathing quickly, her toy-like paws twitching
in dream, dreaming of whatever kittens dream of
in a humidity that softens sound: even the hiss
of trucks braking outside is semi-muted
like the muffled pitch of children at a pool party
squealing underwater.
The act of dwelling within memory
is referred to as 'reflection', as if the past were a stage
with the same set and actors, except the lighting changes
in ways that soften and make golden. By contrast,
the present is lit by overhead fluorescents; artless

and stark as a shopping centre. The general consensus
is that truth eventually becomes obscured
by sentiment. A rosy hue blurs the edges
like a beauty filter that smooths out imperfections.
But what if the gold flecks I now remember floating
in the air around Martin were actually there?
Could it be that the lantern of recollection
illuminates grace and other forces
too subtle to be apprehended
in the austere light of day?

This split second – this jet-lagged moment – fixes my mind on home:
a humane life that's rootless, mindless as summer is.

This summer, I sat by the window
searching the sky for my next line for so long
the season changed. The kitten doubled in size
and ravaged the plants. Great storms howled in.
I saw drenched galahs on twisted powerlines
and lorikeets lashing their wings as if swimming.
When the sun finally emerged from its sabbatical
two kookaburras flew down to the neighbour's aerial.
Bodies bulged like rubber bulbs, they looked straight up
and spoke their magnificent derision.

Half Here

A book about sobriety says I should try to face life on its own terms
but my snarky mind asks what if these terms are unfair?
Seems a bit one-sided, life turning up in its gangster sunnies
and telling you how it's gonna be. Today when I called Mum
she described Grandma's latest mental health crisis.
I'm sorry, she said, *you'll probably have to go through this with me*
one day. Forever an optimist, I told her not to worry
because the apocalypse will arrive before that happens:
I'm banking on it! The prospect of a fiery meteor – one that wipes
us all out instantaneously – cheered her. The author of the book
I'm reading asks: why would anyone want to dull their senses?
Forever a heckler, my mind yelled *because they're relentless!*
Outside my bedroom, cars buzz like amplified beehives
all through the night. For countless years I've been half here,
crouched beside the locked door of the spirit world, squinting
into a thin line of light in search of sense; obsessed. Like Levin
in *Anna Karenina* who found meaning at last while scything a field,
I need to get out of my head. At a book launch last week
the writing life was described as *real losses for imaginary gains*.
On a treadmill at my local gym I set the program to 'rolling hills'
and stared out at the pool where children were learning to swim.
Whenever I see people productively employed in sensible jobs
I think maybe if I were a swim instructor or delivery driver
or supermarket shelf stocker or bagel baker I'd know my place
in the world and find peace. Oh Lord of Chlorine, Gear Sticks,
Forklifts and Cream Cheese, forgive my short attention span.
Grant me a chance to find enchantment in ordinary things.

Notes

Goldsbrough: the epigraph is from ‘Sadness and Isolation’ by Luke Davies.

Golden Repair: the text for the ‘Kintsukuroi’ passage in ‘Golden Repair’ was taken from the Wikipedia entry for *Kintsugi* (a Japanese term which translates as ‘golden joinery’).

We’ll Get Stoned on the Couch if it Takes All Night: the title of this poem was taken from ‘Wallpaper Codicil’ by Peter Minter.

Travels and Travails: ‘less travelled’ is a reference to ‘The Road Not Taken’ by Robert Frost.

Foothills: this poem features excepts from ‘Summer’ by Martin Harrison.

Acknowledgements

Versions of these poems have appeared in the following publications: *Best Australian Poems 2012* and *2015* (Black Inc.), *Communion Arts Magazine* (Walleah Press), *Cordite Poetry Review*, *Make Your Mark*, *Meanjin*, *Other Terrain Journal*, *Pink Cover*, *Poetry d'Amour* (WA Poets Inc.), *Poetry d'Amour 2018* (WA Poets Inc.), *Poetry Listening Lounge* (curated by the Writing & Society Research Centre), *Seizure*, *Velour*, *Westerly* and *ZineWest* (New Writers' Group). 'Amaranthine' was shortlisted for the 2015 Dorothy Porter Prize (*Meanjin*), 'Hot Clouds' was Highly Commended in the 2018 *Overland* Judith Wright Poetry Prize, and 'History of Sadness' was Highly Commended in the 2020 Blake Poetry Prize (delivered by Casula Powerhouse Arts Centre in collaboration with WestWords).

I'd like to acknowledge that these poems were written on the lands of the Gadigal, Dharawal, Dharug, and Gimuy-Walubarra Yidi people, as well as the regions of Tāmaki Makaurau and Whangārei in Aotearoa. I pay my respects to the traditional custodians of these lands and their elders, past and present.

This book was drafted during my doctoral candidature at Western Sydney University, under the supervision of Dr Kate Fagan and Prof. Ivor Indyk. Their support and guidance were crucially important; helping to transform my first attempts into a fully realised collection. Thank you.

I'm also grateful for the support I received from the Writing and Society Research Centre, in particular Dr Melinda Jewell, Dr Fiona Wright and Dr Helen Koukoutsis, who provided editorial feedback, as well as encouragement and inspiration. Additionally, I'd like to extend a special thanks to Varuna, for granting me two writing residencies during my candidature.

Thank you to Assoc. Prof. Sean Pryor and Prof. Ann Vickery, for your close and generous feedback on this collection (as it appeared in my PhD thesis). Thanks also to Luke Davies for taking the time to meet with me in 2015, and for writing the words that changed my life.

Warm hearted thanks to Dr Katharine Pollock, for leading the way with your PhD-to-publication journey, and for being such a gorgeous friend.

To my muse Anna-May Jensen, for filling me with inspiration from all the air in your lungs.

Dr Tamara Schembri, for seeing I had something extraordinary to offer, and providing encouragement despite your near-visceral aversion to poetry. I miss you so much.

Carla Francis, thank you for introducing me to the concept of *Ikigai*, and for being so supportive.

Thanks to the entire Sappho Books crew, with a special shout-out to Cathal Gwatkin-Higson, for your general all-round awesomeness.

To my poetry sister Alice Allan: thank you, thank you, thank you. You are great.

I'm grateful to Steve Broughton for being my best friend during a very difficult time. Your love has nourished me.

Thank you to my aunt Dr Lyndal Carter, for always being there. Thanks also to Mum and (Dr) Dad. And to my sister Megan Carter: you're the best. I love you.

This book is dedicated to the memory of Pamela Carter (1937–2020).

About the author

Louise Carter's poetry has appeared in *Meanjin, Best Australian Poems, Westerly, Cordite* and other publications. Her poem 'Hot Clouds' was Highly Commended in the 2018 Judith Wright Poetry Prize and in 2020 her poem 'History of Sadness' was Highly Commended in the Blake Poetry Prize. She lives on Gadigal land and is a member of the Writing and Society Research Centre at Western Sydney University.